Potty Training

Toilet Train your Child Hassle & Stress Free in a Matter of Days with this 101 Guide!

By Fiona Hathaway

Table of Contents

Copyright

Recording of this publication is strictly prohibited and any storage of this document is not allowed unless with written permission from the publisher. All rights reserved.

The information provided herein is stated to be truthful and consistent, in that any liability, in terms of inattention or otherwise, by any usage or abuse of any policies, processes, or directions contained within is the solitary and utter responsibility of the recipient reader. Under no circumstances will any legal responsibility or blame be held against the publisher for any reparation, damages, or monetary loss due to the information herein, either directly or indirectly.

Respective authors own all copyrights not held by the publisher.

The information herein is offered for informational purposes solely, and is universal as so. The presentation of the information is without contract or any type of guarantee assurance.

The trademarks that are used are without any consent, and the publication of the trademark is without permission or backing by the trademark owner. All trademarks and brands within this book are for clarifying purposes only and are the owned by the owners themselves, not affiliated with this document.

Introduction

Have you ever worried so much about potty training your child because of the time and effort it involves? Let your worries fade because with this guide, you can potty train your little one the hassle-free and stress-free way.

Learn the best tips and tricks on how to potty train your child efficiently within just a matter of days! In this e-book, you will learn about all the things that you need in order to prepare for the training.

Read on to find about the proper way to prepare your child and experience potty training at its easiest and most fun way!

Chapter 1: Signs of Readiness

Before you can begin potty training a toddler, there are signs of readiness you need to watch out for. Potty training a child who is not yet ready will just tire both of you and may even cause setbacks. Below is a list of all the different signs that show that your child is already ready for potty training. If your little one is showing all or most of these signs, then he is ready to be trained.

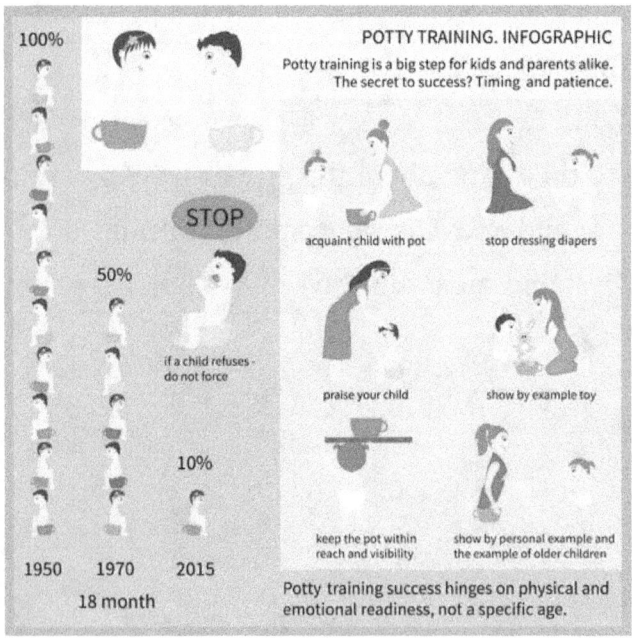

100%

POTTY TRAINING. INFOGRAPHIC

Potty training is a big step for kids and parents alike. The secret to success? Timing and patience.

STOP

acquaint child with pot

stop dressing diapers

50%

if a child refuses - do not force

praise your child

show by example toy

10%

keep the pot within reach and visibility

show by personal example and the example of older children

1950   1970   2015

18 month

Potty training success hinges on physical and emotional readiness, not a specific age.

The following are some of the physical, behavioral and cognitive signs that show the readiness of your child:

Physical Signs

Stays Dry for 3 Hours or More

Babies often have wet diapers when you check on them. As they grow into toddlers, their need to urinate lessens, so they are able to stay dry longer. If your little one can last 3 hours or more without peeing, then it is one physical sign of potty training readiness.

Has a Predictable Bowel Movement

If you are able to predict your child's bowel movement, then it is a signal that you can potty train him soon. This is the time when you already know when to rush him into the potty. He starts to have his own schedule for pooping. You will notice that he usually relieves on certain times of the day. For example, he poops twice:

once at night and once in the morning or afternoon, and no other time; that is an example of a predictable bowel movement.

Runs and Walks Well

A toddler who is able to walk and run well is old enough to be potty trained. Some parents insist that they can potty train their 1 year old, which is not impossible, but rare. The reason why running and walking well is in the checklist is that it determines whether your child has developed coordination, allowing him to handle himself steadily.

Behavioral Signs

Shows Independence

Independence happens when your little one prefers to do things on his own, like drinking from his cup, opening the can of cookies and figuring out his puzzle toy. Taking pride in his own accomplishments is a sure sign of having independence. You will know he thrives for independence when prefers to feed himself or will not take a bite from his biscuit, but wants to hold it himself first.

Hating Dirty Diapers

Babies cry when they need changing, but most of the time, they do not seem bothered. As they turn into 1 year olds, they seem not to care whether they have something of a burden down there because they are more engrossed with playing and exploration. With potty-training-ready toddlers, a dirty diaper is hell. You will know your little one is ready for training when his wet and soiled diaper easily irritates him. It is not an average kind irritation. If anything, it is more of a frustration. Your little one is obviously uncomfortable and turns red and angry about his itchy bottom. They get distracted, bothered and are unable to return to their playing because of constantly scratching at the dirty diaper.

Shows Curiosity of the Toilet

Toddlers do not usually care when you go to the toilet or what you do in there. They only sometimes follow you because they need something, but once they start peeking in and wondering why you are sitting there for so long, it is a sign of growing curiosity. When your little one is growing more curious about the toilet, it means that he is trying to understand what it is for. The more he searches for the importance of this "toilet", the more ready he becomes for potty training.

Verbalizes when He has Soiled his Diaper

When your toddler reaches 2 years of age, he will know and start to use words for peeing and pooping. A more obvious sign of readiness is when your little one is able to tell you, out of the blue sometimes, that he has peed or pooped. Most of the time, toddlers will tell you of their little deed when it is over, but sometimes, they will be able to tell you before or as it happens. The more frequent your little one is able to verbalize his need to relieve himself, the more you can expect to be able to train him for the toilet.

It Becomes Obvious He's Doing his Business

You are not usually able to predict when your child will soil himself, but as he grows older, it becomes more apparent. One sign of readiness to watch out for is when your little one is having a particular behavior or manner before he does his business.

Some of these behaviors include:
- Walking around as if pondering
- Isolating himself from others
- Staying put in one place, longer than he usually does
- Playing while standing up, or refusing to sit his bum down

- Staring in one direction or looking extremely focused
- Grunting, clenching or pursing his lips

Your little one may have his own kind of behavior that is not found above, so you will have to observe what he usually does before he poops. If you see a pattern in his behavior, then that would be a good sign for getting ready.

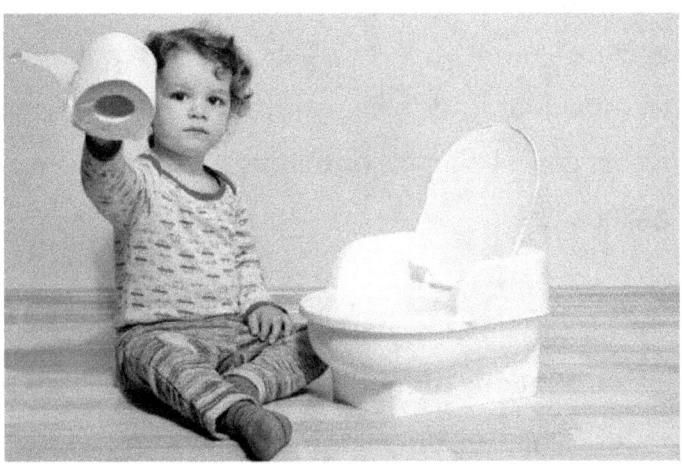

Sits on the Potty Trainer Whenever

 If you have already bought a potty trainer but had it set aside, put it where your little one can see and access it anytime. As it has been said, growing curiosity is one of the main signs of readiness and when your toddler is curious enough, he will occasionally "use" the potty trainer. On random times, or when he feels like imitating you, he will go to the potty trainer, lift up the lid, sit on it and maybe even say "poo poo". His awareness of the trainer's purpose is a great precursor so that he won't be afraid of it in the future. Keeping the potty trainer in sight also helps your little one become familiar with it and feel comfortable about it to begin training soon.

Can Removes his Pants Down or Pull it Up

If your little one is able to pull down his pants on his own, then you can train him to remove it soon when he needs to relieve himself. The reason why he should be able to pull his pants up as well before training is because this indicates that he has now, again, coordination and independence. It is also important in teaching him not to soil his underwear and that deed is for the potty alone.

Can Sit on His Own for 2 to 5 Minutes

One of the biggest challenges most parents encounter while potty training is keeping their child sit still on the potty. An uninterested and irritated child on the potty is not a ready toddler. If your toddler can sit on his own for at least 2 minutes and as much as 5 minutes, then he can last sitting on the potty until his deed is over. Without this particular behavioral sign, potty training can be prolonged or extremely difficult to accomplish.

Generally Cooperative

Toddlers do not always follow your instructions, and sometimes deliberately do the exact opposite of what you ask just to test the boundaries. If your little one is cooperative enough, if not most of the time, he can be potty trained easily. You can teach an obedient or cooperative toddler to stay put or take off his pants when it is time to go. You will be spared from the scene of running after him when he suddenly sprints for the door before he is even done with his business.

Cognitive Signs

Knows the Word for Poop and Knows Its Meaning

If your little one knows the word for poop and what it means, his thinking is well developed enough to know that there is also a calling for every *action*. When your toddler knows the meaning of each action, especially when he is about to go, he is able to interpret or anticipate it when it is about to happen. This is an important precursor to him being able to identify his own needs and therefore tell you of it sooner.

Is Aware of the Physical Signals of Going and Tells

Potty training is best for a toddler who is aware of his body when he has to go. This means your little one can tell that he is about to either pee or poop, and is able to tell you before it happens. Some toddlers will hold it in until you come to the rescue and take him to the potty. This particular cognitive sign is a go signal for potty training. At this point, your little one is able to communicate his needs soon enough for you to be able to give solution to it quickly.

Can Follow Instructions

If your child is able to follow instructions like "Put your toys back in the box," and "Hand me your bag", he will surely be able to cooperate with you. Not only will he be able to do as you teach him during potty training, he will also be able to follow what you ask him *not* to do.

Can Put Things Back in Place

When your little one is able to put things back in place, all on his own, his cognitive function is well developed enough that he understand there is a place for everything. You will know this when he does things like:

- Place his slippers on the rack after using it

- Returns his toys in the box before sleeping

- Puts his dirty clothes in the laundry

- Throws small trash into the bin

- Covers the cookie jar after stealing a treat

Over time, this behavior becomes more of a natural routine and your little one starts becoming aware where each thing belongs. With this knowledge, he will be able to understand that even his little deed has a place and will be able to train himself, with your help, to do it routinely.

POTTY TRAINING. INFOGRAPHIC

Potty training is a big step for kids and parents alike. The secret to success? Timing and patience.

100%

50%

10%

1950 1970 2015

18 month

STOP

if a child refuses - do not force

acquaint child with pot

stop dressing diapers

praise your child

show by example toy

keep the pot within reach and visibility

show by personal example and the example of older children

Potty training success hinges on physical and emotional readiness, not a specific age.

Chapter 2: Potty Training Gear

Earlier generations of parents did not need to use much equipment to potty train their children - us in fact. While their advices are extremely helpful, the aid of certain potty training gears will make your goal easier to achieve than without it. Listed below are key items that you can use to potty train your little one. They are not all required for the training and some might not work for your little one. They are, however, valuable for most parents today. You can always try them first to know which gears would work best for your little one.

Potty Trainers

Described as a small chair-like box with a lid on it, a potty trainer is basically a portable children's toilet. Most potty trainer toilets today are multi-purpose. Some can be turned into small chairs and others even include detachable stairs when the toddler is ready to sit on a real toilet. There are two types of potty trainer toilets, one is a seat and another is a toilet all on its own.

The following Potty Trainer is readily available from Toys R Us.

Potty Trainer Seat

A potty trainer seat is simply just a seat that your little one's bum can fit comfortably on, as opposed to the large seat of an average adult toilet. It should be placed on top of an adult's toilet seat. Ideally, the potty trainer seat is for kids who are big enough to climb and sit on a real toilet, but some younger toddlers are able to potty train with it. You will have to assist your child in using it and may need a stool for him to step on.

The following Potty Trainer Seat is also readily available from Toys R Us.

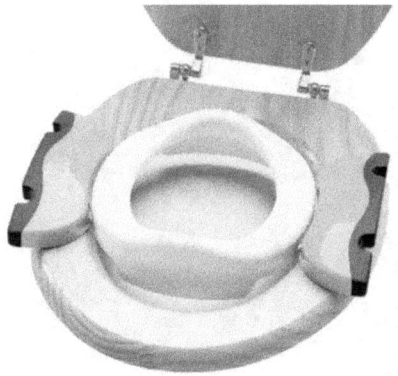

Potty Trainer Toilet

Potty trainer toilets are usually small seats with removable compartments inside. They are designed for a child to use and even feature a lid and sometimes armrests or support. Most potty trainer toilets are colorful or have animal designs to appeal to children. They are useful as substitutes to the toilet in the bathroom. They are efficient because your little one can access it easily and it feels more comfortable than a trainer seat or the toilet itself. You can place it on the floor anywhere in the house and is just the right height or size for your toddler.

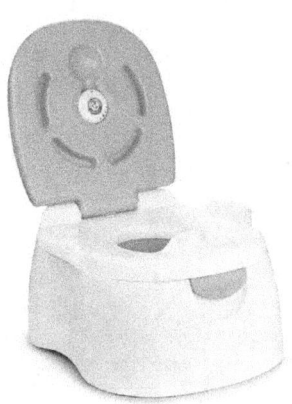

Potty Trainer Pants

For effective potty training, you will have to let your little one run around the house without any diapers. Some parents use potty trainer pants instead, to avoid the mess that goes with that strategy. Potty trainer pants are either a pair of extra thick cotton pants or underwear with a waterproof outer layer. The padding is not thick enough to hold in soil, but is thick enough to last through at least one wet incident. Unlike commercialized diaper pants, trainer pants are washable and therefore less expensive. They are effective enough for toddlers who are extremely sensitive to soiled diapers. It acts as a diaper, but at the same time makes your toddler wary of the absence of one because the underwear is thin enough.

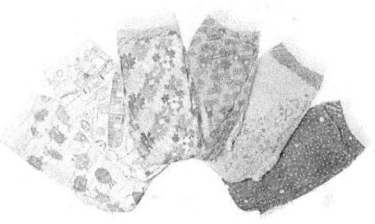

Toddler-Friendly Hand Soap

It is important to teach your little one to wash his hands after doing his business, so toddler-friendly hand soap should be part of your list. It does not have to be a big bottle of soap because no one else but your little one is going to use it. Place it near the toilet or in the bathroom if you prefer to wash your toddler's hand there.

Wet Wipes or Flushable Tissue

One obstacle that parents will experience while potty training is the need to do it while away from home. Having wet wipes in your bag, preferably flushable ones, can really ease the trouble of training your toddler in public restrooms.

Easy Access Clothes

When you are potty training your child, make sure that he has a set of clothes that he can take off easily on his own. Instead of pajamas, have him wear underwear, if not potty trainer pants,

that are loose enough around the waist.
This will allow him to remove his clothing quicker
when it is time to go. Toddlers tend to get
frustrated easily and might get discouraged when
faced with obstacles like a pair of "uncooperative"
pants.

A Stool or Small Chair

As your little one grows older, he will eventually
be able to sit on the toilet by himself, but while
he is still small or when you do not plan on using
a toilet trainer, invest in a stool. It will be a
stairway, literally, for your toddler to reach his
goal, which is the toilet seat. Some toilet trainers
come with portable or detachable stairs for the
same purpose, but are quite expensive. If you
prefer to be economic, then a stool or small chair
to step on will greatly suffice.

Chapter 3: Potty Training the Hassle & Stress-free

Potty training takes a lot of energy and can last for weeks if you do not follow up on your little one or invest enough time into it. Some parents want to avoid the process by letting their kids take the lead, but that would only prolong it and make things more difficult. If you think that potty training is such a hassle, you are right but also wrong. It can be a nuisance if you are doing things wrong, but with the right equipment and strategy, you and your little one can breeze through the process in a week or less!

Signs of Readiness

Once your toddler is showing signs of readiness, you should be preparing yourself as well. By now, you need to start preparing the necessary gears or equipment of your choice for the potty training. Make sure to prepare yourself by setting a date when to start.

Free your week of other responsibilities. This potty training needs some serious focus, but with less time required.

Ready the Equipment

Before starting your potty training session, make sure to have all your equipment in place. Place the potty trainer inside the bathroom, or outside, as long as it is nearby. This will give your little one a general idea of its purpose if you have not explained it to him yet. Have your baby bag well prepared too with wet wipes or disposable tissue inside. Place all other key items like the toddler-safe hand soap and stool within reach or just beside the potty.

Rags and Mopping

It is a sure thing that your little one will not get his potty training right at first. Expect accidents, lots of it. In preparation, have a bunch of rags prepared near key places such as areas where your toddler usually plays and near the bathroom.

Progress Chart

Keeping and using a progress chart will help you to focus on the potty training. It will also help you to keep track of the pattern or changes in pattern of your child's progress. It is also encouraging to see how many days have passed by and how little is left to achieving your goal. A progress chart can help you keep your drive as well because it reminds you of where you left of or are at now. Some examples of progress charts are shown later in this book.

Preparing your Little One

Preparing your little one before starting will cut down the number of days it will take to do the training. Make sure that your child knows the purpose of each equipment or tool you are using and the things you are going to do for the next few days. Your little one is smart enough to understand that activities and changes like these have purposes so explaining it will help him to cooperate more.

Preparing for a Potty Trainer

If you are using a potty trainer, either a seat or a toilet chair, show it to your little one and let him study the thing. Encourage him to sit on the chair, with or without a diaper. If your child ever asks questions about it, answer truthfully, but simply. If it helps, you can dump the contents of his dirty diaper, just to show what it is for and has the same purpose as the toilet in the bathroom.

Preparing for the Toilet

If you plan to settle with the toilet you have in the bathroom, then prepare your little one by allowing him to sit on it with your help, occasionally. Before going in, instruct him to remove his pants and tell him that sitting on the toilet means having to go.

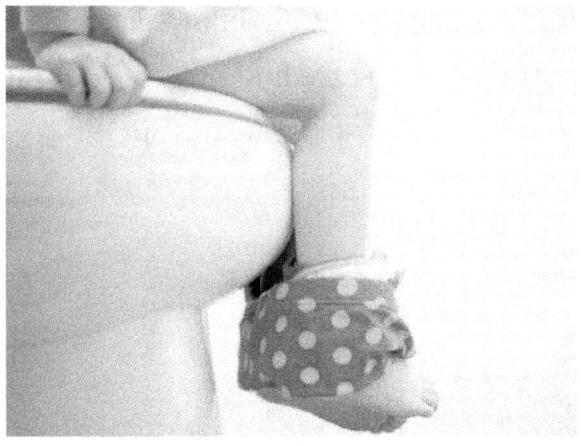

Introduce the Routine

Your little one has to understand that going to the potty will become a routine from now on. First of all, it is becoming more predictable when he will soil his diapers, and that alone has begun a routine. Secondly, making the deed a routine sets the clock on his body. This will encourage a "scheduled" pooping.

 To introduce the routine to your little one effectively, make sure he has become familiar with the potty trainer or toilet first. When he has, start sitting him on the toilet every 15 minutes for 3 to 4 hours. Do this twice - once in the morning and another in the afternoon or evening, depending on when he usually poops. You can do this with or without underwear, of course having no diaper or underwear on would be best.

When to have an all-day session

On the 3rd day of practicing this routine, go on an all-day session. This means you will have to take your toddler to the potty every 15 or 20 minutes the whole day. This is one reason why planning when to begin potty training is important to you. It is also a key strategy in avoiding stress or hassle. You should be able to allot at least two whole days for the sake of potty training alone. Keeping those two days focused on training your little one will greatly lessen the time needed for the potty training.

Naked Time

On the 3rd day or 4th day, let the kid run around the house without underwear. This is best done while you are at home and have no other responsibilities such as errands, so that you can occasionally follow him around.

The point of this strategy is to make your child conscious about himself. It is true that at some point, he will have to go, but during this stage of the training, he is already aware that he will be making a mess without his diapers.

Therefore, when he does need to go, he will come to realize that he needs to find somewhere to put it. He will also be used to visiting the potty already that he may run straight to it to do his business, or simply point at it and tell you. All you need to do now is be nearby to take him to the potty or remind him what to do about it.

Let Him See Where His Poop Goes

Toddlers are curious. When you show them about how things function, they get excited about what they discover. When your little one goes to the potty, make sure that he sees where his poop goes. Tell him that that is where it is supposed to go when he needs to go. Let him flush the toilet, partly for the fun and partly so that he understands that it is the same as putting

things away to their rightful
place.

Show Him How It's Done

When you are the one who has to go, be public
about it to your child. Do it with the door open
so that when your little one passes by he can
peep in. Let him see that adults go to the potty
too. Children at this age like to imitate grown-
ups. Let him ask what you are doing, entertain
his curiosity and just tell or show him all that he
needs to know.

Alert Guardians of the Potty Training

If your little one is already going to school, or if
you need to leave him with either a sitter or a
relative for a day, alert the guardians about his
potty training. It cannot be helped that some
things come up that require you to leave your
child in the hands of others. This does not mean
that you should stop the training abruptly. Alert
others of your little one's progress so that they

can take over and prevent setbacks.

Limit Bedtime Drinks

Training your child not to pee at night is more difficult than teaching him not to soil himself during the day. This particular part of his training takes longer to accomplish, and is often done later on when he is older. To prepare him for night potty training, limit your child's bedtime drinks so he can stay dry for most part of the night.

Bedtime Training is Different

When your little one has had 3 to 4 months of consistent trips to the toilet, he can begin his bedtime training. It is a separate toilet training because he needs to be able to have more control of his bladder first. Children are not very good at controlling their bladder when they are asleep, which makes bedtime accidents difficult to handle. You cannot observe him much at night because it is time to sleep. However, it can help if you let him pee before sleeping. Use wet absorbent pads on the bed if you must. Over time, your child will be able to stay dry through the night.

Read Potty Training Books

Your little one is aware of the changes he is going through. In order for him not to forget about what you are doing, give him picture books about potty training. He will relate well with the colorful pictures and be encouraged to do it. It will reduce any doubts your child may be having about staying on the potty and even make his toilet trips seem exciting.

Accidents Happen

Over the days or even month during and after his training, your little one will have accidents. This is okay, you do not need to stress over it or let your child see that he has failed. Do not, in any way, scold your child for it. If he is aware that he has made a mess, tell him it is okay and remind him that next time, he should tell you when he has to go. Never make him feel bad for having an accident.

It will discourage him from potty training and develop insecurities.

Use a Reward System

Give your little one a reward for every successful trip to the bathroom. Use only small rewards and give them when he has gone through the day without a single mess. You may reward your little one for his efforts, but make sure that he deserves it. Explain to your little one what it is for, and tell him that he can get more when he does well again.

Motivate with Praises

Avoid going overboard when it comes to offering rewards. If possible, use praises instead to encourage your little one to continue the potty training. Children are often more responsive to praises than toys or even food. Because your child has developed a sense of pride, showing him that others appreciate his accomplishments motivates him to repeat it.

Chapter 4: Reward Ideas for Effective Motivation

One ideal strategy in potty training is giving your little one a reward after a successful deed on the toilet. The reward will encourage your child to repeat the accomplishment. This can also boost his pride. It will also give him one more reason to look forward to and exert an effort in accomplishing his toilet trip. Below are ideas on the type of rewards you can use to encourage your little one during his potty training.

Food Prize

Children love tasty snacks so it is no wonder that a small snack, like a piece of cookie, is perfect as a reward for efforts. After a successful, or almost successful, potty training session, give your little one a piece of cookie or chocolate coupled with praises for his effort. Use food that he rarely sees at home or is not usually allowed to have in large amounts.

This does *not* include junk food, sodas, potato chips and candy.

Sodas and junk food are bad for your child's health especially if they get used to it. Introducing these kinds of food at an early age will make them search for it and crave for it, which is not a very healthy habit. If you want, you can use healthy, non-MSG potato chips for your reward system. Ice cream could be also given on special occasions, which means once or twice at most during the whole potty training session. In any case, never use candy because your little one can easily choke on it. Use small pieces of chocolate instead, preferably organic ones.

Stickers for Success

If you do not see food as a healthy or ideal way for rewarding your child's potty training success, you can always use items like stickers as prizes. Kids love cartoons.

They like seeing drawings of their favorite characters on tables, on TV, on their bags, on their plate and even on their arms. To show your little one he has done a great job on his potty training session, reward him with a little sticker of his favorite cartoon on his hand. Along with praises, put on the sticker while telling him it is for his cooperation on the potty training session.

Art Crafts

You probably are expecting toys as items to use for this particular reward system. On the contrary, using new toys to encourage your child during potty training sessions might only spoil him or increase his expectations. Using toys as a reward will not just make your toddler think he will get more even after the potty training. It is also expensive.

Toys as rewards are too much since potty

training usually only lasts a week at most, if done properly. To save money and not risk spoiling your toddler, use art crafts instead. You do not need to buy them. In fact, you can do them on your own and keep them stored so your little one will not see them right away.

The art crafts you can do should be simple and small like:

- Origami of animals or flowers

- Small Paper Doll

- Paper Lantern

- Paper or Plastic Masks

- Craft Boats

- Sailboat, Birthday and King or Queen Hat

- Easter Egg (Decorated Egg shell or Boiled Egg)

Reminders

Here are a couple of reminders on food prizes:

- Give food prizes in small amounts; preferably one piece for each successful toilet trip.

- Wash your child's hands before giving the prize.

- Never use or offer junk food.

- Emphasize that it is a prize and not a meal, so he will not expect more.

- Give it with praises.

Ways to record Successes and Failures

Very Simply using your computer and a printer you can create a fun way to record your son's or daughters potty behavior.

Boys Potty Behavior Chart

Girls Potty Behavior Chart

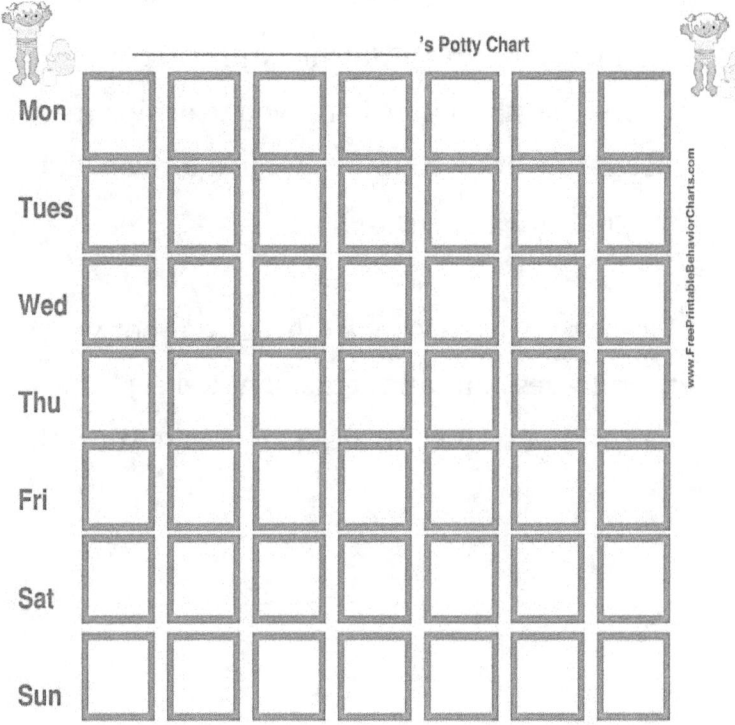

There are many more similar types of charts available freely in the Internet.

Conclusion

Thank you again for downloading this book! I hope that this guide helps you to achieve a stress-free potty training, not just for you, but for your little one as well.

Please refer to this book during your potty training sessions and remember to keep motivating your child as you motivate yourself!

www.ingramcontent.com/pod-product-compliance
Lightning Source LLC
Chambersburg PA
CBHW071355310526
45790CB00017B/1043